Hi, this is Sylvia.

D0287032

Hi, this is Sylvia.

I can't come to the phone right now, so when you hear the beep, please hang up.

by Nicole Hollander

St. Martin's Press, New York

HI, THIS IS SYLVIA. Copyright © 1983 by Field Enterprises, Inc. Copyright © 1983 by Nicole Hollander for material on pages 5 and 23 and at the bottom of pages 24, 25, 50, 51, 80, 81, 104, and 105. All rights reserved. Printed in the United States of America. No part of this book may be used or reproduced in any manner whatsoever without written permission except in the case of brief quotations embodied in critical articles or reviews. For information, address St. Martin's Press, 175 Fifth Avenue, New York, N.Y. 10010.

Design by Tom Greensfelder

Library of Congress Cataloging in Publication Data

Hollander, Nicole.
  Hi, this is Sylvia.

  I. Title.
PN6728.S97H59   1983   741.5'973   83-2999
ISBN 0-312-37193-4 (pbk.)

First Edition

10 9 8 7 6 5 4 3 2 1

tHis Book is ^lovingly DEDICAtED to my other cat, Harriet, WHO SELDOM APPEARS IN tHE SYLVIA StRip.

TODAY U.S. NATURALIZATION AND IMMIGRATION AUTHORITIES ROUNDED UP OVER A HUNDRED WOMEN

WHO ARE SUSPECTED OF HOLDING JOBS USUALLY FILLED BY MEN.

THE WOMEN WERE GIVEN A CHOICE OF CLERICAL WORK OR DEPORTATION.

FILM AT 11:00

12

MR. JOHNSON, CAN YOU DESCRIBE YOUR HEADACHE FOR US?

YES. IT FEELS LIKE EIGHT LINEBACKERS, WEARING THEIR SPIKES, TAP DANCING ON MY HEAD.

NO! WAIT A MINUTE; ACTUALLY IT FEELS LIKE MY HEAD IS CAUGHT BETWEEN TWO ROCKS, BEING SLOWLY FORCED TOGETHER BY A HUGE, SLOBBERING BEAR.

THOSE ARE THE WORST KIND.

GRUNELLA, THIS VACATION IS GOING TO BE TERRIFIC.

BEACHES OF WHITE SAND, MOONLIGHT ON THE WATER, PIÑA COLADAS, ROMANCE...

SHARKS!

SHARKS! YEECK!

YES. I SEE THEIR SLEEK BODIES GLIDING THROUGH THE WATER... THEIR SHARP WHITE TEETH—THEIR BLONDE HAIR AND THEIR CORUM WATCHES.

ALL RIGHT!

BE CARE-FUL.

Sylvia On Sunday

14

25

16

AS YOU KNOW, JUDY HAS LEFT ME

I WAS SORRY TO HEAR ABOUT IT, RAEMON.

MARRIAGE FACILITATOR

I AM, OF COURSE, BROKEN-HEARTED, BUT I AM A MAN WHO MUST BE MARRIED.

RAEMON, I'M SURE YOU'LL LOVE AGAIN SOMEDAY

SYLS SPECIAL SERVICES

THE BAND HAS BEEN HIRED, AND tHE MINISTER AND THE CATERER ARE ON THEIR WAY.

PHYLLIS, ARE YOU FREE THIS AFTERNOON?

THE DEVIL tRIES tO MAKE A DEAL WITH A VERY NEGAtIVE MAN.

IN EXCHANGE FOR YOUR SOUL, I CAN GIVE YOU ETERNAL LIFE.

OH SURE, SO I CAN KEEP MAKING THE SAME MISTAKES OVER AND OVER AGAIN. DO YOU KNOW WHAT THAT'S LIKE? NO, OF COURSE NOt. GUYS LIKE YOU NEVER KNOW WHAT IT'S LIKE FOR GUYS LIKE ME.

I WONDER IF MY THERAPIST IS AWAKE.

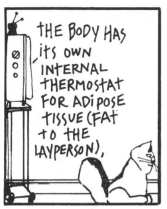
THE BODY HAS its OWN INTERNAL THERMOSTAT FOR ADIPOSE TISSUE (FAT to the LAYPERSON),

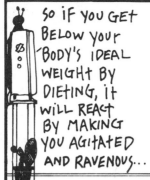
SO iF YOU GET BELOW YOUR BODY'S IDEAL WEIGHT BY DIETING, it WILL REACT BY MAKING YOU AGITATED AND RAVENOUS...

UNTIL YOU EAT ENOUGH to GET BACK to its IDEAL WEIGHT.

SO ACTUALLY MY THERMOSTAT ORDERED ALL THIS CHINESE FOOD.

Hi! I'M DR. ETTA BRADLEY, PSYCHOLOGIST AND PROFESSIONAL NEWSPAPER READER, WITH A SPECIAL ½ PRICE OFFER.

ARE YOU A DEPRESSED BUSINESS MAN WITH HIGH BLOOD PRESSURE? ARE YOU AFRAID TO READ THE WALL STREET JOURNAL? DO YOU FEEL EACH DOW-JONES WILL BE YOUR LAST?

LET ME DO THAT READING FOR YOU! EVERY MORNING I'LL CALL YOU WITH A SUMMARY OF BUSINESS NEWS AND HOW IT AFFECTS YOU.

LIKE I MIGHT CALL AND SAY: "It's O.K. BABY, YOU'RE STILL IN BUSINESS." OR: "SOMEONE WENT DOWN THE TUBES, BUT IT WASN'T YOU." CALL OUR TOLL-FREE NUMBER.

GREAT LIES: Samson and Delilah

AiEEE!

ACTUALLY IT WAS SAMSON WHO GAVE DELILAH THAT FAMOUS HAIRCUT. IT'S REPORTED THAT DELILAH ASKED FOR A TRIM, AND INSTEAD GOT ONE OF THE WORST HAIRCUTS OF THE PRE-CHRISTIAN ERA. IN A BLIND RAGE SHE DESTROYED THE SALON AND A NEARBY BOUTIQUE.

MRS. JONES, LET'S DO A BLIND TASTE TEST.

TRY THESE TWO COFFEE CAKES AND TELL ME WHICH ONE YOU LIKE BETTER.

THEY'RE BOTH DISGUSTING.

THE QUEST FOR THE HOLY GRAIL AND OTHER ANXIETY PRODUCING METAPHORS

HAROLD.
I'M LEAVING
TO LOOK —
FOR MY
"G" SPOT.
KISS THE
CHILDREN
GOODBYE
FOR ME.

DENVER

fragment
OF A
LETTER
from
Mae
West
to Helen
Gurley
Brown

Dear Mouseburger,
I'm beyond
"G"...

Hi this is Bernice; I
can't come to the Phone
right now; I'M LOOKING
FOR MY "G"
SPOT.

 WANNA BAT?

27

SYL, YOU WILL NOT BELIEVE THE **DAY** I HAD YESTERDAY— FIRST THE DISHWASHER QUITS, THEN THE COOK DECIDES HE'S GOING TO BE A MOONIE, OR A REPUBLICAN, OR SOMETHING, AND HE SPLITS...

SO JESSICA AND I ARE DOIN' EVERYTHING, AND BY LUNCHTIME IT'S A MADHOUSE IN HERE, AND THEN THESE TWO WEIRD-LOOKING GUYS WALK IN.

SO ONE OF THE GUYS SAYS: "THIS IS A STICK-UP, GIVE ME YOUR MONEY **NOW**."

SO I SAID: "IF YOU'RE IN A HURRY, GO TO MCDONALDS"

RUBY, I HATE TO MENTION THIS, BUT THERE'S SOMETHING BIGGER THAN A BREADBOX IN MY SOUP.

MA, THIS BUDGET NEEDS TRIMMING.

IT'S BARE BONES, RITA.

WHAT ABOUT THIS ITEM: "ORCHIDS"?

THAT ITEM IS FIRM...

TAKE OUT "FOOD!"

"THE UGLY JEWELRY EXCHANGE" DO YOU HAVE A LOT OF JEWELRY AROUND THE HOUSE THAT YOU NEVER WEAR?

WHEN YOU OPEN A DRAWER AND YOU'RE LOOKING FOR SOMETHING ELSE, DO YOU ALWAYS COME ACROSS A LARGE, MOSS GREEN BAKED ENAMEL MALTESE CROSS, WITH A BIG EMERALD CUT BROWN STONE IN IT, AND YOU SAY: "HUH! WHAT WAS I THINKING OF WHEN I BOUGHT THIS?" WELL I BELIEVE THAT SOMEWHERE IN THIS GREAT LAND OF OURS, SOME WOMAN IS LONGING FOR THAT MONSTROSITY, AND FOR A SMALL FEE, IT WILL BE MY PLEASURE TO BRING THE TWO OF YOU TOGETHER.

McDONALD'S ANNOUNCED THE ADDITION OF A NEW SANDWICH TO ITS POPULAR "McRIB" AND "McCHICKEN" LINE.

FOOD NEWS WITH PATTY

THE NEW PRODUCT WAS CREATED IN RESPONSE TO THE TIGHTENING BUDGETS OF FAST FOOD LOVERS.

THE SANDWICH WILL SELL FOR 50¢ AND WILL BE CALLED "McBREAD."

DO YOU KNOW WHAT THE OLDEST QUESTION IN THE WORLD IS?

IT'S "WHAT'S FOR DINNER?"

I THOUGHT IT WAS: "WILL THIS BE CASH OR CHARGE?"

37

39

Sylvia On Sunday

OKAY, YOU TALK, I'LL TYPE.

PHOTOGRAPH OF VENUS, WITH BLURRED FIGURE OF A VELOUR AT THE FAR LEFT.

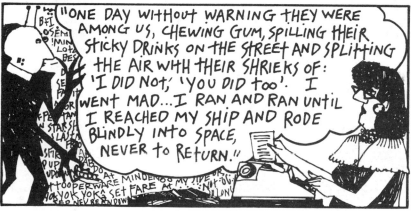

two PeoPLe WHo Are ASKiNG for trouBLe

I NEVER HAVE ANY MONEY... CAN'T DO ANYTHING, CAN'T GO ANY-WHERE. I HATE IT!

WAIT A MINUTE! YOUR SHIP IS ABOUT TO COME IN.

GOOD NEWS! YOUR SHIP IS ENTERING THE HARBOR.

WHAT'S THIS??

AMERICAN TEA LEAF READINGS

SOME HIDDEN SHOALS?

A GYPSY IS RIGHT MORE OFTEN THAN A STOCKBROKER. — GRUNELLA

IT SUNK.

TIPS

DON'T BLAME ME.

SCIENTISTS ANNOUNCED TODAY THAT PEOPLE WHO EAT FOODS CONTAINING A HIGH PERCENTAGE OF PRESERVATIVES

MAY FIND THEIR BODIES

LIVING LONGER THAN THEY DO.

THIS STATION APOLOGIZES FOR ANY INCONVENIENCE CAUSED BY

NEWS BRIEF

OUR EARLIER ANNOUNCEMENT

OF A SOVIET INVASION.

IT'S BEEN A SLICE: INSPIRED BY REAL LIFE THIS FASCINATING BOARD GAME STARTS WITH EACH PLAYER SPINNING THE DIAL TO DETERMINE THEIR GAME STATUS.

THE PLAYER WHOSE SPIN LANDS HIM ON "RICH" GETS ALL THE CHIPS AND PROPERTY. THE PLAYER LANDING ON "POOR" GETS A FAULTY SPACE HEATER.

THE SYLVIA SCHOOL OF WRITING EXERCISE 476 COMPLETE

THE FOLLOWING PARAGRAPH:

"I COME IN PEACE", SHOUTED ARAKO TO THE CURSED METAPHOR PEOPLE WHO SURROUNDED HIM, WHINING AND PRODDING HIM WITH THEIR POINTED PTHOES. "WAIT," HE CRIED, "I HAVE BROUGHT BACK THE SACRED TALISMAN..."

AND SO SAYING, HE BROUGHT OUT A JADE BOX CONTAINING:
1. A BIC LIGHTER
2. A CONVENTIONAL NUCLEAR WEAPON.
3. OTHER.

HARRY, THIS BOOK IS FASCINATING. IT'S ABOUT REAL MEDICAL MYSTERIES SOLVED BY DOCTORS AND PUBLIC HEALTH INVESTIGATORS.

SOME REAL BIZARRE DISEASES IN THIS BOOK.

DON'T READ IT.

TRUST YOUR PRESIDENT.

OH MY GOD. I'VE GOT ANTHRAX!

I KNEW IT.

49

WE COULD DO it.

WE COULD SURVIVE A NUCLEAR ATTACK. PEOPLE COULD TURN THEIR REC. ROOMS INTO BOMB SHELTERS,

AND THEN IN A FEW YEARS, THEY COULD TURN THEM BACK INTO REC. ROOMS. AND INVITE A FEW INSECTS OVER FOR POKER.

54

Sylvia on Sunday

THERE'S A CERTAIN COMMERCIAL, YOU KNOW THE ONE I MEAN, THAT LIKE, IF I HEAR IT ONE MORE TIME I WILL TURN INTO A RAVING MANIAC.

LITTLE BOBBY LOOKS JUST LIKE YOU; HE'S GOT "RING AROUND THE COLLAR" TOO.

ZOTT!

ZOTLE!

57

58

At a news conference today, the President again chastised the media for their "slanted" coverage of administration policies, here and elsewhere.

He asked reporters to trust his version of events, and to put themselves in his hands.

Some reporters wept openly at his criticism, while others were quite rude.

They were out of kitty coq au vin.

RING! RING!

RING RING

Hi, this is SYLVIA. I can't come to the PHONE RIGHT NOW,

5 YR. DIARY

BUT I'D LIKE TO TAKE THIS OPPORTUNITY TO TELL YOU THE DETAILS OF MY RECENT ORAL SURGERY.

IN KEEPING WITH HIS EFFORTS TO REPLACE GOVERNMENT HANDOUTS WITH VOLUNTARY CORPORATE GIVING,

THE PRESIDENT UNVEILED A PLAN IN COOPERATION WITH MAJOR RETAILERS TO...

ALLOW POOR OLD PEOPLE TO SHOPLIFT FROM 2 TO 3 EVERY THURSDAY AFTERNOON.

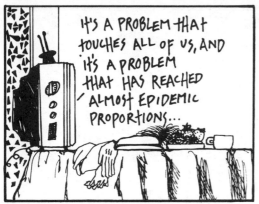

IT'S A PROBLEM THAT TOUCHES ALL OF US, AND IT'S A PROBLEM THAT HAS REACHED ALMOST EPIDEMIC PROPORTIONS...

IT'S SEXUAL "BURNOUT"

OH GOOD, I'M TIRED OF INFLATION.

SNAKE STORIES AND LAME EXCUSES VOL. 2

OLD WIVES TALES

TALL STORIES

I CAN'T COME; I HAVE TO WASH MY HAIR.

NO, HONEST I'D LOVE TO COME, BUT I CAN'T GET AWAY.

THE SYLVIA SCHOOL OF WRITING: VOCABULARY ENHANCEMENT. PICK THE SENTENCE WHICH USES THE WORD GOTH (GŎTH) CORRECTLY.

□ SHE HATH GOTH WHAT IT TAKES.
□ GOTH, IS THAT A MUSHROOM-SHAPED CLOUD?
□ WHAT ARE YOU, SOME KIND OF GOTH?
□ IS THAT A GOTHIC SPORTSCAR?

YOU SEE A MAN ACROSS A CROWDED ROOM. AN AMPHITHEATER? NO! IT'S A SUPERMARKET.

YOUR EYES LOCK. SPARKS FLY! YOU DISCOVER MUTUAL INTERESTS IN THE FROZEN FOOD SECTION YOU HAVE YOUR FIRST QUARREL NEAR PET SUPPLIES.

YOU RECONCILE PASSIONATELY AT THE DAIRY CASE, BUT BREAK OFF AT THE CHECKOUT COUNTER.

SO HE DOESN'T EVEN CARRY MY GROCERIES TO THE CAR!

WAIT! THE STORE MANAGER IS SHOWING SOME INTEREST.

SYLVIA ON SUNDAY

Sylvia's Children
a Soap Opera in Doctors

SCENE SWITCHES TO KEN AND NURSE ANNE IN HAPPIER TIMES. IN SLOW MOTION WE SEE THEM RUNNING ON THE BEACH, PLAYING WITH A FRISBEE, AND IN FRONT OF A ROARING FIRE.

DARLING, WE'LL BE LIKE THIS FOREVER!

OH, KEN, WILL WE REALLY FIND HAPPINESS THIS TIME?

SCENE OPENS IN THE O.R. OF A CITY NEAR NEW YORK. THE ATMOSPHERE IS TENSE. THE SURGEON GESTURES FOR THE SCALPEL. HIS NURSE APPEARS NOT TO HEAR HIM... THE SURGEON KICKS HER TO GET HER ATTENTION. SUDDENLY SHE COVERS HER FACE WITH HER HANDS AND CRIES OUT: "I CAN'T DO IT!"

I LOVE KEN TOO MUCH TO HELP CUT HIM OPEN.

GET AHOLD OF YOURSELF, NURSE ANNE!

GAS

THAT LITTLE MINX! CAN'T STAND IT THAT KEN'S THE CENTER OF ATTENTION.

TOO TRUE.

LOOK, IF I CAN HANDLE MYSELF IN A PROFESSIONAL MANNER, SO CAN YOU—AFTER ALL HE IS MY SON, EVEN IF HE DOESN'T KNOW HE IS.

BACK TO O.R.

NURSE BETTY

YOUR SON! HOW COULD HE BE YOUR SON? I'M HIS MOTHER, AND I'VE NEVER DONE IT WITH YOU!

BETTY, REMEMBER WHEN YOU CAME BACK FROM THE BRAZILIAN JUNGLE AND YOU HAD A RAGING FEVER AND THEN YOU WENT INTO A COMA? IT WAS THEN THAT WE HAD OUR AFFAIR.

WAIT A MINUTE... I CAN'T KEEP QUIET ABOUT THIS ANY LONGER!

PHYL.

WHAT HAS PHYLLIS BEEN KEEPING UNDER HER CAP?

69

THE STORY CONTINUES...

THIS WEEK NURSE PHYLLIS TRIES TO TELL HER SECRET.

I WANT TO TELL, COM'ON, LET ME TELL.

UPDATE: DURING AN OPERATION TO REMOVE A BOTHERSOME BRAIN IMPLANT FROM KEN FOSTER, NURSE ANNE BREAKS DOWN AND REVEALS THAT SHE STILL LOVES KEN; DR. PALMER THE SURGEON REVEALS HE IS KEN'S REAL FATHER, WHICH COMES AS RATHER A SURPRISE TO NURSE BETTY, WHO IS KEN'S MOTHER.

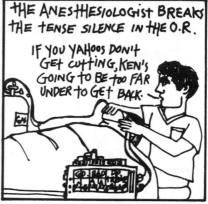

THE ANESTHESIOLOGIST BREAKS THE TENSE SILENCE IN THE O.R.

IF YOU YAHOOS DON'T GET CUTTING, KEN'S GOING TO BE TOO FAR UNDER TO GET BACK.

BETTY, YOU'RE NOT REALLY KEN'S MOTHER. MY SISTER PHOEBE IS KEN'S REAL MOTHER. SHE WAS IN THE HOSPITAL, DELIVERING HER BABY AT THE VERY SAME TIME YOU WERE DELIVERING YOURS.

NO KIDDING?

YOUR BABY DIED; I SWITCHED BABIES, AND GAVE YOU PHOEBE'S BABY, KEN. I WAS PRETTY ANNOYED WITH PHOEBE AT THE TIME AND FIGURED THIS TRAGEDY WOULD MAKE HER LEAVE TOWN.

WELL AS LONG AS IT'S TRUTH-TELLING TIME; I'D LIKE TO TELL SOMETHING TOO.

OH, HEY, MAN! DON'T TELL THEM THAT.

71

THIS IS PATTY MURPHY TALKING WITH A 109-YEAR OLD MAN ABOUT ANXIETY.

SO STAN YOU'RE SAYING THAT MOST OF OUR ANXIETIES CAN BE TRACED DIRECTLY TO SPECIFIC FOODS OR CHEMICALS.

YES, PATTY. FOR INSTANCE MONEY WORRIES ARE CAUSED BY REFINED SUGAR. —

73

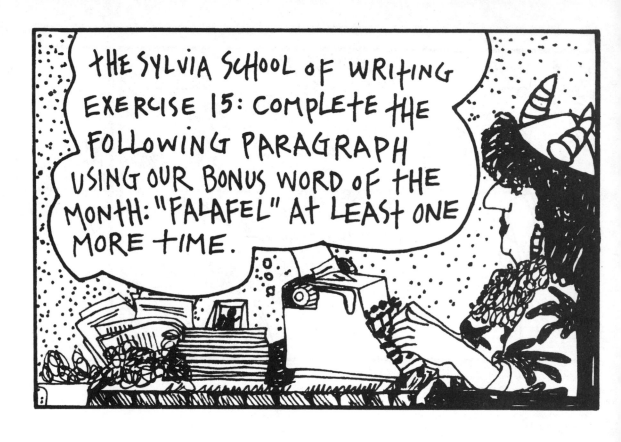

WHEN YOU'RE OVER-WEIGHT, DRESS AS SIMPLY AS POSSIBLE. AVOID RUFFLES, FRILLS, AND BOLD PATTERNS.

THAT'S ONE THEORY.

I HATE THE PHONE.

RING RING RING

RITA, I WANT TO BE BURIED WITH THIS PHONE.

RING

THEN WHEN IT RINGS, I'LL BE ABLE TO IGNORE IT.

RING

YEAH, WHAT D'YUH WANT?

THE WASHINGTON PRESS CORPS WAS STUNNED TODAY WHEN PRESIDENT REAGAN SUGGESTED MUD WRESTLING AS A SUBSTITUTE FOR AFFIRMATIVE ACTION.

A STAFF AIDE SAID LATER THAT THE PRESIDENT HAD MISUNDERSTOOD THE QUESTION, BUT REFUSED TO SAY WHAT QUESTION THE PRESIDENT THOUGHT HE WAS ANSWERING.

TODAY, FOLLOWING NEW YORK'S LEAD, BANKS ALL OVER THE COUNTRY

FINANCIAL NEWS WITH PATTY.

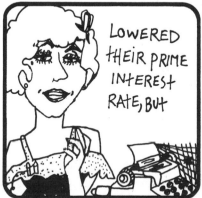

LOWERED THEIR PRIME INTEREST RATE, BUT

RAISED THEIR SERVICE CHARGE ON BOUNCED CHECKS TO $520.00

AND HERE WITH AN OPPOSING VIEW TO OUR RECENT EDITORIAL ON THE NUCLEAR FREEZE MOVEMENT IS GERNIF, A MEMBER OF "CONCERNED VENUSIANS FOR THE PLANET EARTH."

Ā LŪVLĒ PLⁿⁿt̄ ⊙⊜⊙

NOMR̈ WAAR, PĒĒCĒ UN ERt!

HE'S SO ARTICULATE.

I HAVE THIS RECURRENT DREAM OF BANANAS... DANCING, DANCING, AND THEN I'M IN A TUNNEL AND I SLIP ON THE BANANA SKINS AND I TRY TO GRAB THE WALL,

BUT THE WALL IS ALIVE AND I TRY TO RUN AND I CAN'T, AND THEN I LOOK DOWN AT MY FEET...AND THEY'RE WEBBED.

SYLVIA ON SUNDAY

SOME MIDWESTERNERS BEGIN TO WORRY ABOUT WINTER RIGHT AFTER LABOR DAY; OTHERS ARE CAUGHT BY SURPRISE EACH YEAR.

WHAT THE HELL IS IT?

ITS SNOW, DEAR.

SOME HAVE VISIONARY PLANS.

IN MY SPARE TIME, I AM DIGGING A TUNNEL TO SOUTHERN CALIF. IN 7½ YEARS, I WILL BE ABLE TO RIDE MY BIKE COMPLETELY UNDERGROUND FROM HERE TO THERE.

SOME PEOPLE ACHIEVE A DEGREE OF COMFORT IN THE WINTER BY LETTING THE HAIR ALL OVER THEIR BODIES GET LONG.

THE MEN IN MY FAMILY HAVE ALWAYS USED THIS METHOD. WHEN WE GET BALD, WE MOVE TO FLORIDA.

SOME CURTAIL THEIR SOCIAL LIFE.

DURING THE SUMMER MONTHS, I MAKE PRESERVES OF ALL KINDS. DURING THE WINTER, I STAY HOME AND EAT THEM.

SOME PEOPLE GO AROUND IN GROUPS TO KEEP WARM.

CAN THIS MARRIAGE BE SAVED?

I LOVE WINTER; IT MAKES ME FEEL ALIVE! THE COLD AIR IS INVIGORATING, AND SNOW MAKES DRIVING AN ADVENTURE.

WE'LL BE AT MY MOTHER'S

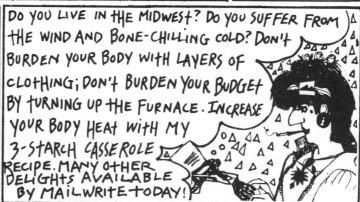

DO YOU LIVE IN THE MIDWEST? DO YOU SUFFER FROM THE WIND AND BONE-CHILLING COLD? DON'T BURDEN YOUR BODY WITH LAYERS OF CLOTHING; DON'T BURDEN YOUR BUDGET BY TURNING UP THE FURNACE. INCREASE YOUR BODY HEAT WITH MY 3-STARCH CASSEROLE RECIPE. MANY OTHER DELIGHTS AVAILABLE BY MAIL. WRITE TODAY!

87

TODAY THE STATE OF WYOMING ANNOUNCED

FINANCES WITH PATTY

THAT BECAUSE OF PRESSING FINANCIAL DIFFICULTIES,

THEY ARE CONVERTING THE STATE INTO A SINGLES BAR.

SWEETIE, I'VE JUST GOT A FEW ITEMS; CAN I GET AHEAD OF YOU?

BUT THAT'S NOT FAIR.

BAKING SPICES

LITTER

OF COURSE YOU'RE RIGHT, BUT SOMETIMES I GET SO TIRED, WHAT WITH THE GRANDKIDS AND MY JOB AND THE HOUSEWORK, AND...

OH HEY, I'VE GOT MY CAR, CAN I GIVE YOU A LIFT? A COKE?

89

90

Lives of Susan

Comedy mini-series about a woman who has a 3-way split personality: Waitress, Housewife, and Brain Surgeon.

IN THIS EPISODE SUSAN, IN HER PERSONA AS A BRAIN SURGEON, SLIPS WITHOUT WARNING, INTO HER WAITRESS PERSONA AND BEGINS TO SERVE COFFEE AND RYE TOAST DURING THE OPERATION. LAUGHS GALORE WHEN SHE BERATES THE PATIENT FOR NOT LEAVING A BIG ENOUGH TIP.

HARRY, IT'S NOT THAT I DON'T LIKE TO TRAVEL; I DON'T LIKE TO PACK. I ALWAYS TAKE THE WRONG STUFF.

REMEMBER LAST TIME I WENT ON A TRIP, I PACKED A HALTER TOP AND 2 PAIRS OF SHORTS,

AND EVERYONE WAS WEARING DOWN JACKETS.

CHICAGO'S ALWAYS CHANCY IN MARCH.

92

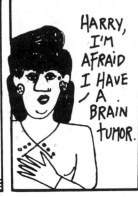

96

HARRY, HERE'S ANOTHER STORY ABOUT A WOMAN WHO WENT TO A BAR TO HIRE A MAN TO KILL HER HUSBAND.

HARRY, DO YOU REMEMBER WHEN PEOPLE CAME TO A BAR FOR A FEW DRINKS AND A LITTLE COLOR T.V.?

I DON'T REMEMBER ANYTHING BEFORE PAC-MAN.

THE SYLVIA SCHOOL OF WRITING EXERCISE 17: COMPLETE THE FOLLOWING PARAGRAPH USING OUR BONUS WORD OF THE MONTH "TITHE" (TĪTH) AT LEAST ONE MORE TIME.

"WHERE ARE ALL MY TITHE AND SHIRTS," HE YELLED. I SQUIRMED WITH GUILT; I HAD GIVEN HIS TITHE TO THE CHURCH AND HIS SHIRTS ALL HAD "RING AROUND THE COLLAR." _____

101

102

103

107

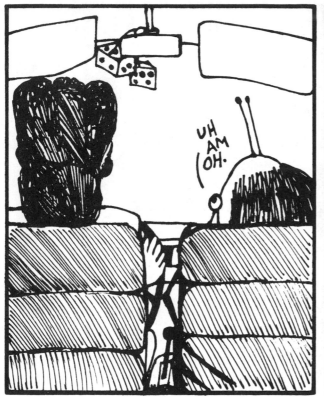

108

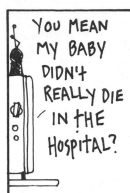 YOU MEAN MY BABY DIDN'T REALLY DIE IN THE HOSPITAL?

 IT REALLY WAS JENNIE'S BABY THAT DIED, BUT YOU AND MARCO SWITCHED BABIES,

AND YOU GAVE MY BABY TO JENNIE?!!

 WELL, IT SEEMED LIKE A GOOD IDEA AT THE TIME

 TODAY PRESIDENT REAGAN OFFERED TO DEBATE RUSSIAN PRESIDENT BREZHNEV ON AMERICAN TELEVISION.

 "THE DEBATE WOULD SETTLE ONCE AND FOR ALL WHICH IS BETTER: DEMOCRACY OR COMMUNISM;

 IT'LL BE SORTA LIKE THE PEPSI TEST," SAID A WHITE HOUSE SPOKESMAN.

A cat being cured of Hairballs through a television Ministry

place your right paw on the screen

213

Hi, this is Patty Murphy talking with Dr. Etta Bradley, psychologist and bon vivant, about a little-discussed urban syndrome.

Dr. Bradley, is it fair to say that you view people who are dependent on public transportation as neurotic?

Patty, if we analyze our relationship to public transportation using the same standards that we apply to personal relationships, the true nature of that relationship is revealed.

If you had a friend who never showed up on time, who often left you standing on street corners in snow and freezing rain and who was always asking you for money—and if you kept on waiting for that friend on those same corners—people would rightly conclude that you were sick.

But Dr. Bradley, people have to use the bus to get to work.

Work is a neurotic dependency.

115

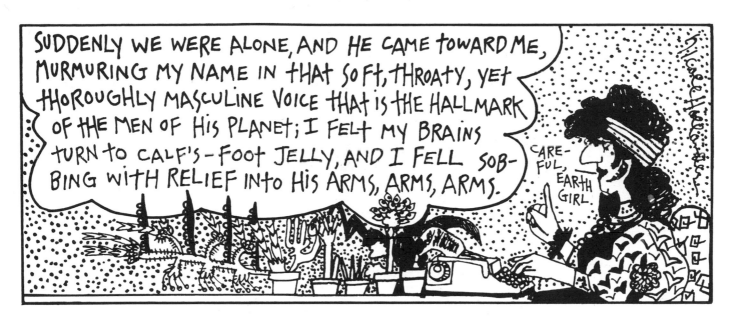

At his press conference today, the president again insisted that he is sensitive to the poor,

THE POTOMAC SCENE

and that in fact several of them are living in the White House basement.

A presidential aide said later that the president had been speaking metaphorically.

THE SYLVIA SCHOOL OF WRITING: WORD OF THE WEEK: "TOKEN"

Complete this sentence: "Here is a token of my esteem," he said, handing her _____.

A. Bus fare
B. A middle management position.
C. A funny cigarette.

123

124

125